13. 20

The Origins of Wisdom

CHIVALRY

O. B. DUANE

First published in Great Britain in 1997 by
Brockhampton Press,
20 Bloomsbury Street,
London WC1B 3QA
A member of the Hodder Headline Group.

ISBN 1 86019 550 4

A copy of the C.I.P. data is available from
the British Library upon request.

Produced for Brockhampton Press by Flame Tree Publishing,
a part of The Foundry Creative Media Company Limited,
The Long House, Antrobus Road, Chiswick, London W4 5HY

The Origins of Wisdom

CHIVALRY

O. B. DUANE

BROCKHAMPTON PRESS

Foreword

ᛞᛟ

'THE KING STABLYSSHED ALL THE KNYGHTES, and gaff hem rychesse and londys; and charged them never to no outerage nothir morthir, and allwayes to fle treon, and to gyff mercy unto hym that askith mercy . . ., and allwayes to do ladyes, damesels, and jantilwomen and wydowes socour . . . and never to enforce hem, uppon payne of dethe. Also, that no man take no batayles in a wrongfull quarrel for not love ne for no worldis goodis . . .'

So Sir Thomas Malory, writing in the middle of the Wars of the Roses when the nobility of England was engaged in destroying itself with little thought for those noble ideals he imagines King Arthur imposing on his knights. Malory's nostalgia is for a time that probably never was. But it is a fact that the early middle ages saw not only a thorough redefinition of terms and concepts — like kingship and knighthood — that we might easily think unchanging but managed to attach to them and to their practice a morality to which, in some measure at least people adhered and nobody could ignore. The use of force, the abomination of war, was made subject to a code of values to which many subscribed; and it is beyond doubt that the condition of human life in Europe was made better than it would otherwise have been.

This short book admirably introduces the reader to the complex history of the development of chivalry, from the ideology of the comrades in arms of the Germanic war band of the early Middle Ages to the elaborate etiquette of the tournaments of the High Middle Ages. It introduces the problems of personal morality and the codes of love, once seen as the proper and refined diversion of the knight. We are the distant heirs of those values and inhabit a world, the history of which has been partly formed by them. They still matter, if only to help us explain facets of our behaviour that we take for granted.

Dr C. W. R. D. Moseley, Director of Studies in English, Wolfson College, Cambridge
January 1997

A chivalric knight would take up any challenge, quest or contest to win a lady's hand.

Contents

ଚ୍ଚଓ

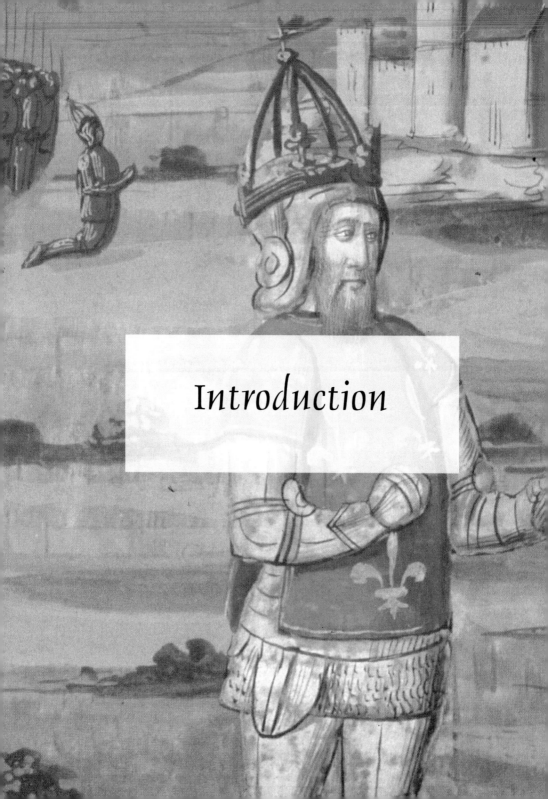

Introduction

Introduction

☙❦

Affability, courtesy, generosity, veracity, these were the
qualifications most pretended to by the men of arms,
in the days of pure and uncorrupted chivalry.

Bishop Hurd, Letters on Chivalry and Romance (1762)

THE MOST LIKELY IMAGE to spring to mind at the mention of the word
'chivalry' today, is one of the perfect gentleman — an impeccably mannered indi-
vidual who displays gentle and courteous behaviour, especially towards women.
Combing our way through history in search of the beginnings of this social code,
we may safely trace it back to the Middle Ages. This was an era which nurtured
the ascendancy of a mail-clad cavalry, at first simply a military force, yet later
evolving into a powerful fraternity espousing principles of honourable and gallant
behaviour hitherto unheard of in European society on any grand scale.

The word 'chivalry' has its earliest roots in the French word for horse,
cheval, and a knight in that same language is called a chevalier, the ambassador of
la chevalerie (chivalry). Indeed, many social historians consider knighthood and
chivalry to mean one and the same thing. Originally, however, the chevalier was
simply a horseman equipped with lance and sword for battle, a barbaric descendant

Sir Percival succeeded in the Quest for the Holy Grail as the worthiest and purest in heart of all the knights.

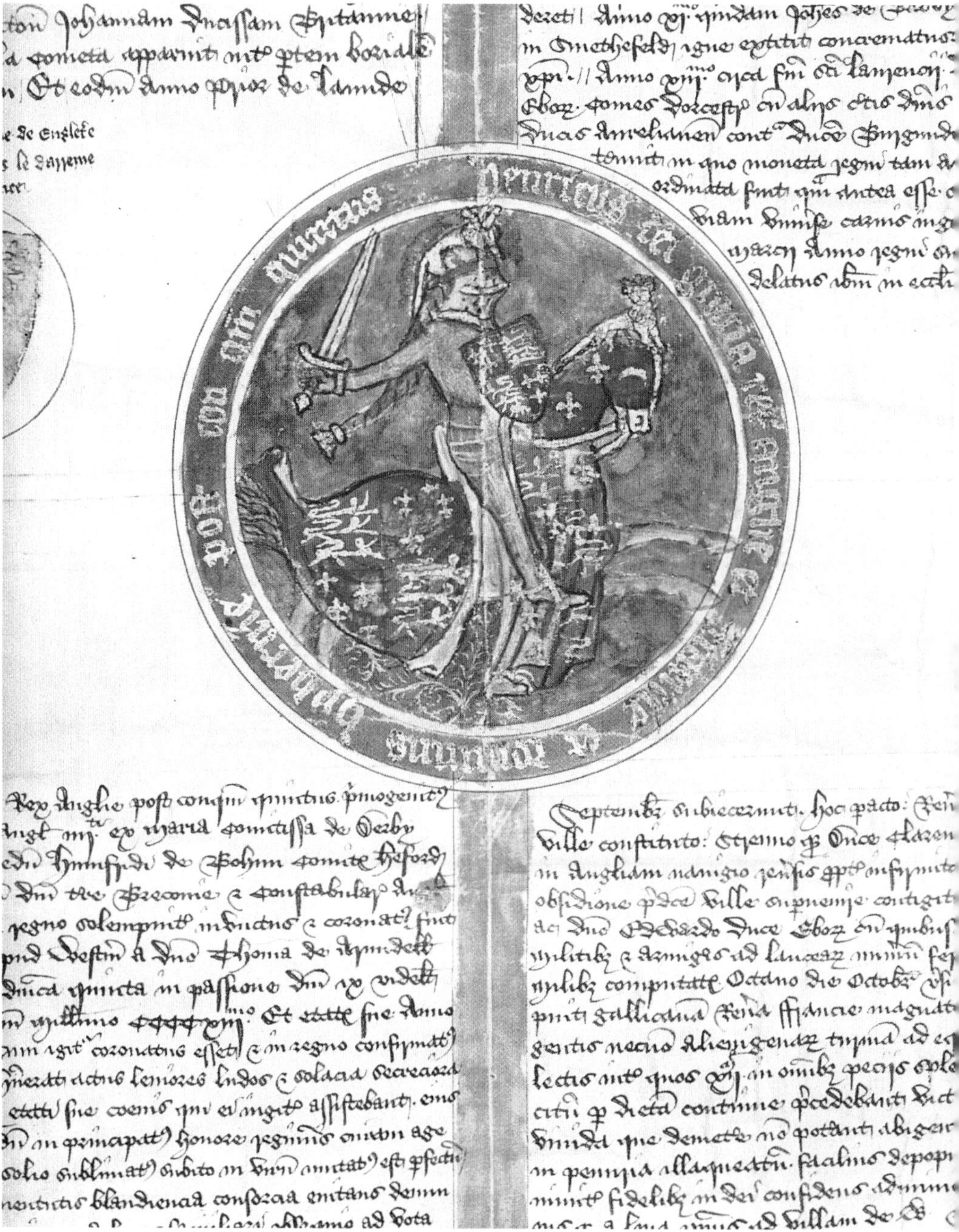

of the Germanic Goths who raided and invaded the Roman Empire from the third to the fifth centuries. As time progressed, the knight's image grew in sophistication, and by the end of the eleventh century knighthood had come to denote a person of noble birth, often possessing property, whose responsibility it was to uphold certain religious, moral and social systems.

No one may assign a precise date to the birth of chivalry, but it is generally agreed that it was at its height between the eleventh and thirteenth centuries, falling into decadence and decline during the fourteenth, ultimately to become a subject of unbridled farce in the fifteenth century.

A KNYGHT there was and that a worthy man
That from the tyme that he first bigan
To riden out, he loved chivalrie,
Trouthe and honour, fredom and curteisie.
Ful worthy was he in his lordes werre,
And therto hadde he riden, no man ferre,
As wel in cristendom as in hethenesse,
And evere honoured for his worthynesse.

Geoffrey Chaucer, Prologue to the Canterbury Tales (c. 1390)

Henry V was one of the greatest warrior knights, leading many successful campaigns.

In the attempt to evaluate its importance to the evolution of Western civilization, critics are sharply divided. Some have called it 'the most glorious institution that man himself ever devised'[1], and 'that splendid institution which threw its lustre over so many ages of gloom and anarchy'.[2] Others, however, condemn its glorification of war for its own sake, its contempt for social inferiors, and its 'picturesque mimicry of high sentiment, heroism, love and courtesy'.[3]

This book neither challenges nor defends these arguments. Its simple purpose is to provide an introduction to the subject of chivalry, mapping the birth, development and decline of an institution which flourished magnificently for a brief period only, yet whose influence lives on today.

Now that his armour was clean, his helmet made into a complete head-piece, a name found for his horse, and he confirmed in his new title, it struck him that there was only one more thing to do: to find a lady to be enamoured of. For a knight errant without a lady is like a tree without leaves or fruit and a body without a soul.

Cervantes, *Don Quixote* (1605)

[1] G. P. R. James, *History of Chivalry*.
[2] H. Stebbing, *History of Chivalry and The Crusades*, Edinburgh 1830
[3] J. R. Green, *Short History of the English People*.

Legends tell of courageous deeds undertaken by knights in order to win the favour of maidens fair.

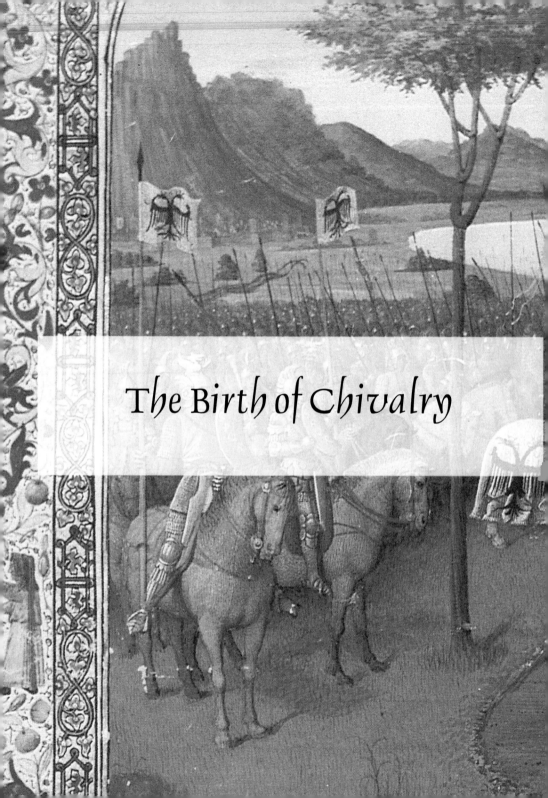

The Birth of Chivalry

The Birth of Chivalry

❦❦

Roland has passed through the gates of Spain, on Veillantif, his fine fast horse. He is wearing his arms, which suit him well; but he has his lance in his hands, and goes twirling its point against the sky, with the pure white banner laced at its tip; its golden tails flap down against his hands.

La Chanson de Roland, c. 1090

The Beginnings of Chivalry

UNDER THE INFLUENCE OF THE CHRISTIAN CHURCH towards the end of the eleventh century, knighthood underwent a noble transformation from military institution to glorious profession, giving rise to an era when the chivalric spirit was in its prime. But in tracing the origins of chivalry, some historians insist that we must reach a great deal further back in time — to the rude but wholesome customs of the ancient Germanic tribes who overran the Roman Empire.

St George, shown here with the slain dragon at his feet, embodied all the qualities of a chivalric knight.

Writing in the first century of the Christian era, the Roman historian Tacitus has provided us with a description of these tribes which, some would argue, has much in common with the system and spirit of later medieval knight-hood. 'The noblest youths', writes Tacitus, 'were not ashamed to be numbered among the faithful companions of a celebrated leader, to whom they devoted their arms and service.' Indeed, war was enthusiastically embraced by these nomadic tribes, and having attained military age, the youth born of free parents swore allegiance to his chief and was publicly presented with spear and buckler, belt and sword as a form of knightly initiation. 'In the hour of danger,' adds Tacitus, 'it was shameful for the chief to be surpassed in valour by his companions, shameful for the companions not to equal the valour of their chief. To survive him, if he fell, was irretrievable disgrace. To protect his person, and to increase his glory by their own triumphs, were the most holy of their duties.' All knights who belonged to this class of freemen were also originally equal, a concept which was maintained throughout the period of medieval chivalry.

Chivalry, then, may be defined as the moral and social law and custom of the noble and gentle class in Western Europe during the later Middle Ages, and the results of that law and custom in action.
F. W. Cornish, *Chivalry*, 1901

Prior to the rise of knighthood as a chivalric profession, the valour of a knight was tested by displays of military prowess.

Er commance lucan enfuiuant fa ma
tiere de Cefar fon fecond liure et Deufe com
ment cefar et fes fegions partirent de fauerne
et fen vindient fur le fleuue De Fubicon J.
nant Cefar qui adontques eftoit
en fauerne atout fon oft ouyt la
nouuelle que le fenat auoit
Refufee la Requefte que les tu
buns faifoient pour lui Et que les tribuns
eftoient xxxxxxx De partis par De la Cite
De Romme Il fift tantoft appareille toutes
fes femione et les emmena tout coyement De
la Cite De fauerne que les citoiens ne auoy
euffent que il voulfift emuar Romme et fon
route Car ceroir fiz le feuffent Il le voul
iffent Retenir et prendre comme ceulx qui
eftoient De la puiffance De Romme Et pour

mieulx fauoir la chofe Il ala auecques les Ci
toiens au teatre pour feliarder les commune
ment De laville Et ala Regardant vne gant
place ou Il deuoit fait edifier vui cercle ou
les chaualliers aux efpees fe combaroient en
laqufe qui eft Venfee ca amuee. Anee ala
Cefar fouple: pcomme il auoit acoufume quant
Il et fait appareiller Renceuoment fon aine De
vui four et fen Veftit m oun eftoit xefc fon hoftel
et fuent les milles hen dome au aue et bien
atelle. Il monta fus et fen vfft De la ville par
vui feret fentier atout vui De compaignie
et cen tant apres que chandelles fuent eftaitee
que Il trouua vui ruceu xes le Iour par qui
enfaugnement Il fui auoir Et auft fe fu emba
tu en vui Deftour xone Il comint que Il et les
fiene uffiffent tout apte m auoit poini De

A further characteristic of the Germanic tribes which anticipates the chivalric spirit of the Middle Ages was the profound respect they showed towards their women. The nomadic tribes treated their women in a manner approaching religious veneration and considered marriage a sacred bond. Chastity was placed on a par with heroism, and men consulted their women on every important occasion, seeking their advice and support in times of battle.

It was the Goth who learned the use of cavalry in his conflict with the Romans, asserting himself as 'the lineal ancestor of all the knights of the Middle Ages'[1] as he unleashed his fierce conquering spirit upon the disciplined infantry of the enemy. An eye-witness account of the Goths in battle dating from AD 470 also conforms, in many respects, to our image of the medieval knight at arms:

'... they wore high, tight, and many-coloured garments which hardly reached down to their bare thighs ... Their swords hung down from their shoulders on baldricks, and round their waists they wore a belt of fur adorned with bosses ... In their right hands they held barbed lances and throwing axes, and in their left shields, on which the light shone, white on the circuit and red on the boss, displaying both opulence and craftsmanship.'

Europe in Turmoil

Often described as the Dark Ages, the early Middle Ages saw the decisive collapse of the great Roman Empire, as hordes of Northern barbarians, including Vandals, Visigoths and Ostrogoths, descended upon the plains of Gaul, Spain and Italy, subduing and dividing amongst themselves the kingdoms they encountered and destroying the Roman system of imperial administration. What followed were centuries of lawlessness and chaos, interrupted only by the illustrious, yet overly ambitious, reign of Charlemagne. For even when the restless Teutonic tribes

Women in this time were regarded as objects of veneration, and were treated with respect and courtesy.

ceased to be nomadic, their warlike disposition remained active and alive. Once the Romans ceased to be a threat they began to cross swords with each other, fighting to gain control of land.

Renewed turmoil followed the dissolution of Charlemagne's great empire. Petty kingdoms were established by the greediest and most powerful; each lord or chief assumed the importance of a prince and became a law unto himself; and everywhere the strong oppressed weaker members of society. All this led to the creation of a system of government throughout Europe known as feudalism.

Feudalism

The feudal system, in which fiefs — holdings of land to maintain a lord and his household — were granted by important overlords in exchange for military support in times of crisis, was properly established during the Carolingian period as the most effective means of protection against repeated aggression by bands of plunderers. It was at this juncture that the 'knight' began to emerge as the dominant military force, although far from being the perfect gentleman serving as an ambassador of chivalry. It would be more appropriate to describe him as a bloodthirsty soldier, compelled by circumstance and by the terms of his tenure to equal the barbarity of his aggressor.

Opposite: Charlemagne, shown on the left in full armour, ruled successfully in a turbulent era of war and destruction.
Overleaf: The early knight was a ruthless and aggressive military figure, far removed from the gentleman knight of later times.

Dant lempereur charlemai
gne eut cõquises toutes ces
terres ⁊ ces estrãges cites et
chasteaulx sans nõbre de lu=
ne mer iusques a lautre par laide de nřēpř

⁊ les eut soustraictes des mains aux mescre
ans ⁊ cõuerties en la foy xpienne si cõme li
stoire a deuãt parle. Il fut moult trauaille⁊
debrise de grãs osts quil eut tãt de fois con
duis sur les ẽnemis ⁊ des grãs trauaulx

A knight should be bold, fair, courteous and well-mannered, generous and loyal, not foolish or rash, and should speak fairly without discourtesy. A knight should be all this, and also proud and fierce to his enemies, and kind to his friends.

Durmart, lines 12129–36, c. 1210–40

The feudal 'knight' of the early Norman period, both in England and on the Continent, was a vassal who held his land in return for his readiness to accompany his lord into the battlefield. More frequently than not his overall conduct was marked by ferocity and lack of restraint. He was a bandit, a thief and a violator of sacred orders. Something needed to be done to elevate the knight from barbaric savage to nobleman by adding purpose to his profession — something which could not remain the responsibility of those few fighting lords sick and weary of the suffering they witnessed around them. Fortunately, the solution was close at hand. The Church began to promote the marriage of war and religion, and it was as a result of the Christian Crusades, which achieved this union, that medieval chivalry came into bloom.

[1]   Oman, *History of the Art of War.*

The Christian Crusades managed to change the role of knighthood. From being a lawless violator the knight became a purposeful nobleman.

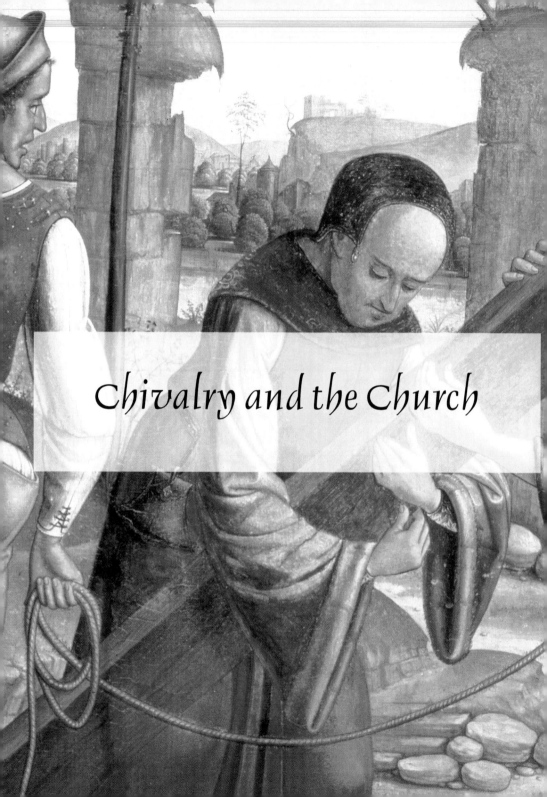

Chivalry and the Church

Chivalry and the Church

⊗

Safe is the battle in which it is glorious to conquer and a gain to die. Why do you hesitate, you servants of the Cross. Why do you, who want for neither strength nor good, make excuses? ... I ask and advise you to put the business of Christ before everything else and not to neglect it for what can be done at other times.

Saint Bernard of Clairvaux, Letter to Duke Wladislaus and the nobles of Bohemia (c. 1130)

IN THE DAYS OF THE ROMAN EMPIRE, the Christian Church had adopted a pacifist stance in face of aggression, but during the centuries which followed, Christendom was increasingly compelled to defend itself with the very weapons used against it. The rise of Islam in the East during the seventh century — a religion which ruled by the sword — marked the first real turning point in the Church's attitude to war. As the city of Jerusalem fell and Christians suffered the most appalling persecution, churchmen began to re-examine their views. In Europe, ecclesiastical authority was at an all-time low and the Church was spared

Opposite: Chivalry began to focus on the teachings of the Church as the foundation for its moral code.
Overleaf: Religious persecution led to harsh warfare between the Christians and the Turks.

none of the violence of secular warfare. Monasteries and churches suffered repeated looting and destruction, monks were put to death and nuns were burned in their convents. By the end of the eleventh century, the Byzantine Empire was seriously weakened and much of its former domains in Asia Minor was in the hands of the aggressive and intolerant Seljuk Turks. Christianity had entirely reversed its attitude to force, and sought to mobilize itself militarily as fast as possible. The idea of warring against the forces of darkness is common: St Michael the Archangel destroying the dragon sanctions military force, and Christ himself is sometimes portrayed as a young warrior. Crucial to this rethinking of Christian values and perspectives, and of military force, was St Paul's image of the Christian as soldier in *Ephesians* VI.

> **Wonderful sights were to be seen. In the Temple of Solomon, men rode in blood up to their knees and bridle reins. Indeed it was a just and splendid judgement of God that this place should be filled with the blood of unbelievers since it had suffered so long from their blasphemies.**

Raymond of Aguilers, History of the Franks who Captured Jerusalem, c. 1102

The Crusades offered the chivalric knight the opportunity of ultimate sacrifice in the service of Christianity.

Mindful of her interests both at home and abroad, the Church saw that she could use the feudal 'knight' to her own advantage: these undisciplined, hot-tempered military men could satisfy their great thirst for war and adventure while saving Christendom from extinction. A Crusade to the Holy Land would join them together in meaningful enterprise. They would serve as the champions of a new Christian chivalry, they would 'ride together redressing human wrongs', they would sacrifice themselves to a noble ideal of service for the glory of God.

The Crusades

The first Crusade was proclaimed in 1095 by Pope Urban II at the Council of Clermont in France. 'A people without God,' he exclaimed, 'the son of the Egyptian slave, occupies by force the cradle of our salvation — the country of our Lord.' Every person of noble birth, it was urged, should take a solemn oath before a bishop that he would 'defend to the uttermost the oppressed, the widow and the orphan.'

Although it remained a sin to kill Christians, a pilgrimage to the Holy Land involving the slaughter of the 'Saracen infidels' who attacked Christ's sacred tomb would be quite acceptable in the sight of God. As a reward for this great work, knights would receive plenary indulgence upon their return to Europe. Peter the Hermit's passionate preaching boosted the cause. His fiery enthusiasm urged hordes of followers, not just the nobility, to unite in a common bond of knighthood against the foe, and to recover from the hands of disbelievers so many objects dear to the souls of the faithful.

Go forward in safety, knights. With undaunted
souls drive off the enemies of the cross of Christ
... How glorious are the victors who return from
the fight! How blessed the martyrs who die in
battle!

Saint Bernard of Clairvaux (preacher of the Second Crusade, 1146)

The People's Crusade

The First Crusade, which became known as the People's Crusade, was not quite what the Pope had foreseen, however. The call to arms was taken up by a far greater portion of the peasantry than the Church would have liked. Full of savage passion and ignorant faith, the undisciplined rabble marched eastwards, massacring Jews in the Rhineland, attacking and pillaging Hungary and Bulgaria until, finally, they were ambushed and slaughtered themselves by the Turks in Asia Minor.

Christian chivalry was yet in its infancy, but slowly, through the Church's refusal to abandon its crusading ideal, it began to assume a more definite aspect, and by the time the official army of the First Crusade travelled to Constantinople the following year, the nobility rather than the peasantry dominated the ranks. For now, as the century drew to a close, it was the custom for every noble father to educate his son in the orders of knighthood. The Crusades continued and the

great Crusading Orders were established — the Hospitallers, the Templars and the Teutonic Knights. By the early twelfth century, the Church had begun to take control of the ceremony of knightly investiture. Religion had succeeded in consecrating knighthood to that most lordly vocation every young man of gentle birth longed to follow.

All your blood you must shed in defence of Holy Church.

L'Ordène de Chevalerie, late twelfth century

The Knight's Education

A boy with ambitions to be a knight had to undergo a thorough training which usually began at the age of seven. Parental tenderness was judged an obstacle to his education, and so the child was taken from his home and placed in the service of a neighbouring lord, himself a fully-fledged knight. Here, in the pursuit of chivalric honours, the boy took up his office as page. He was taught implicit obedience to the wishes of his lord and lady. He served them at table, he learned to ride, and he accompanied his lord on various excursions. It was left to the lady of the manor to develop the gentler aspects of the boy's character. She schooled him in the basic rules of chivalry, discussed love and religion with him and supervised his musical training.

At the age of fourteen, the page was usually promoted to the higher grade of squire. During a religious ceremony, he exchanged his dagger for a manly sword

By the end of the eleventh century, it was the custom for every noble father to educate his son in the orders of knighthood.

and received moral instruction on its correct usage. His duties now were far more varied and challenging. He became proficient in the use of sword, lance and battle-axe.

He took care of his lord's armour, followed him to war, supplied him with fresh arms, dragged his body from the battlefield if he fell, and buried him if he were killed.

At the age of twenty-one, if he had served his lord well, the squire was judged eligible to receive the honour of knighthood. Many squires, however, remained devoted to their lords an entire lifetime.

It is not without reason that the soldier of
Christ carries a sword; it is for the chastisement
of the wicked and for the glory of good.

Saint Bernard of Clairvaux, Letter to the Knights of the Temple

Ceremony of Knighthood

That a knight's sword should uphold the dignity of the Church was central to the notion of Christian chivalry and it was considered only proper that the ceremony which elevated him from the position of squire should be rich in religious symbolism. The young man was expected to fast the day before his initiation and to spend the night in prayer. On the following morning, he was stripped of his

Opposite: *Women played an important role in the education*
of the young knight, schooling him in the gentler laws of chivalry
Overleaf: *In this painting, Botticelli depicts a stylized image of a warrior knight in the Middle Ages*

clothing and taken to a bath which was representative of his purification. He was then dressed in a red robe (emblematic of the blood to be shed in the course of duty), and over this robe was placed a black doublet – symbol of his mortality and that of all mankind.

After the high mass had been chanted the young aspirant approached the altar and handed his sword to the bishop or priest. It was laid upon the altar and blessed with the clergyman's prayer:

'Hear, God, we beseech thee, our prayer, and, with the right hand of thy majesty, deign to bless this sword, wherewith thy servant desires to be girded, that it may be the defence and protection of churches, of widows, orphans, and all who serve God, against the cruelty of Pagans; and that it may be powerful, and a fear and terror to all deceivers, through Jesus Christ.'

The religious part of the ceremony having been completed, the candidate was led before the lord who intended to knight him. Once he had given a satisfactory response to the questions which challenged his motives in demanding the honour of chivalry, he was granted his knighthood.

The Ceremony of Knighthood was a solemn religious occasion requiring a great deal of physical and moral preparation.

The nineteenth-century French historian and archivist Léon Gautier outlined the code of ethics embraced by the medieval knight as follows:

I   *Thou shalt believe all that the Church teaches and shalt obey all her commandments.*

2   *Thou shalt defend the Church.*

3   *Thou shalt respect all weaknesses and shalt constitute thyself the defender of them.*

4   *Thou shalt love the country in which thou wast born.*

5   *Thou shalt not recoil before thine enemy.*

6   *Thou shalt make war against the infidel without cessation and without mercy.*

7   *Thou shalt perform scrupulously thy feudal duties, if they be not contrary to the laws of God.*

8   *Thou shalt never lie, and shalt remain faithful to thy pledged word.*

9   *Thou shalt be generous, and give largesse to everyone.*

I0 *Thou shalt be everywhere and always the champion of the Right and the Good against Injustice and Evil.*

Léon Gautier, The Decalogue, or Ten Commandments of Chivalry

After the religious part of the Ceremony of Knighthood, the young aspirant knelt to receive his accolade.

Tournaments

From the twelfth to the sixteenth centuries tournaments were held regularly and played an important part in the training of young men. Every nobleman was expected to take part and, in spite of resolute opposition from the Church — due to the high death toll of participants — the popularity of tournaments was overwhelming. Etiquette was rigid and many rules were modelled on romantic fiction of the day: a knight would joust for the love of his lady — often to the death. Winners gained great honour, as well as riches, and before long regular rounds of tournaments began to take place throughout Europe, with reigning stars who competed habitually.

Ostensibly a form of entertainment, tournaments were very useful training for battle strategies, resulting in highly skilled warriors for the crusades.

Chivalry required that youth should be trained to perform the most laborious and humble offices with cheerfulness and grace.

Kenelm Digby, *The Broad Stone of Honour* (1822)

The rules and etiquette of tournaments were rigid and a knight would often fight to the death.

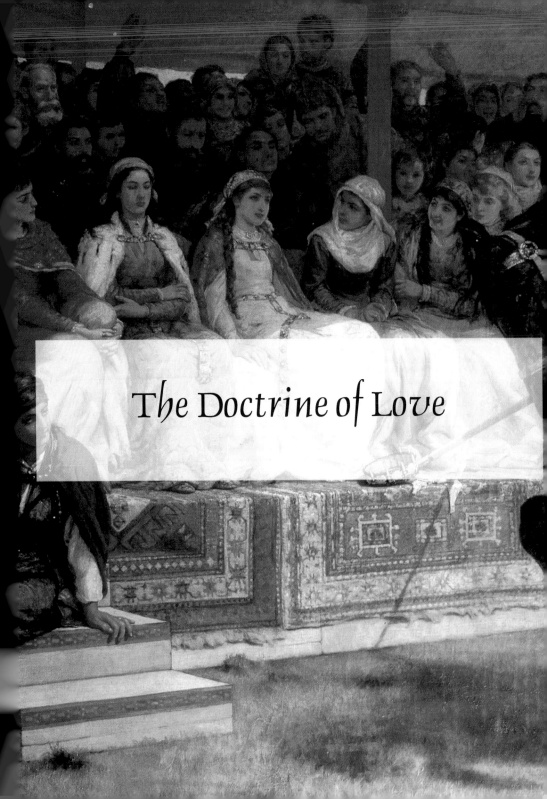

The Doctrine of Love

The Doctrine of Love

&Q&

And, indeed, he seems to me
Scarce other than my king's ideal knight,
Who reverenced his conscience as his king;
Whose glory was, redressing human wrong;
Who spake no slander—no, nor listened to it;
Who loved one only, and who clave to her.

Alfred Lord Tennyson, The Dedication—Idylls of the King (1859)

IT HAS BEEN SAID of the age of chivalry that no higher ideal of sexual relations has ever been put forward than that which the best of the knights professed and practised. But, as we have seen in the previous chapter, the first chivalric knights, the Christian Crusaders, were strictly devoted to their Church and to the concept of noble warfare, leaving themselves precious little time for the worship of fair ladies. Gradually, however, a new doctrine began to evolve, a doctrine of gallantry, which considered itself equal, if not superior, to both war and religion as a vehicle of chivalric conduct.

The highest glory of any knight was to be worthy of the love of the lady he desired.

The Influence of the East

From the outset, the Church remained suspicious of the code of gallantry which infiltrated Christian chivalry, believing it distracted the knight from the worthier task of rescuing the Holy Land from the infidel. But the Church proved powerless to prevent gallantry from establishing itself securely as a crucial element of chivalry. The repeated journeys made from Europe to the Holy Land in the name of the Crusades had the effect of introducing knights to the unfamiliar customs of other nations. In Eastern Christendom they discovered a respect for women they were unaccustomed to in the West. In Constantinople they discovered the splendour of Eastern luxury and a great love of ceremony. In Arab society, which was strongly influenced by the Persians, they encountered evidence of a more spiritual union between man and woman, together with a passion for music and poetry. Many knights came to appreciate what they saw and carried these influences back to Western Europe with them.

... no knight can be brave unless he is in love; love gives the knight his courage.

Lecoy de la Marche, A. La Chaire française au moyen âge, Paris 1886

The ideal of chivalric love developed out of the poetry and songs carried through Europe by Troubadours.

The Role of the Troubadour

The spirit of Arabic love poetry filtered up through Spain, still largely Moslem, to the Christian states of Catalonia, Aquitaine and Provence in Southern France. It found receptive soil in a society that already admired the witty love poetry of the Roman poet Ovid. The combination of these two strands, and the resulting interest in the psychology of love and the ironies of the situation of lover and beloved — the one dying (so he said) of desire and the other unattainably, almost divinely, aloof — framed the new poetry of Europe. The driving force of this art was the virtue of selfless service and courtesy to ladies and women — what the German minnesingers called Frauendienst — intermingled with exaggerated, yet enchanting, accounts of the chivalric exploits of knights at war. The troubadours, as they came to be known, a breed of minstrel-soldier responsible for the spread of this new poetry, began to flourish as a species, having a major effect on the evolution of social manners throughout Europe and the subsequent development of all European lyric poetry.

Their high feast was Love, who gilded all their joys; she brought them King Arthur's Round Table as homage and all its company a thousand times a day! What better food could they have for body or soul? Man was there with Woman, Woman there with Man ... They had what they were meant to have, they had reached the goal of their desire.

Gottfried von Strassburg, Tristan (c. 1210)

It became a favourite pastime of kings, knights and their ladies to compose their own poetry.

Just from seeing his countenance, his great beauty and his appearance, he has all their hearts with him, so that all the knights, ladies and maidens dread him coming to harm.

Chrétien de Troyes, Erec et Enide, c. 1170

As the twelfth century progressed, knights errant and troubadours were welcome everywhere. Poetry became the favourite pastime of the age, and a form of brotherhood evolved which considered all poets equal, regardless of birth. The art of composition was practised by kings, knights and ladies, as well as by professed poets and wandering minstrels. The romans, fabliaux, chansons de geste and ballads of southern and central France were recited and imitated throughout Europe, gradually becoming more elaborate in style.

And ever the more Sir Gareth beheld that lady, the more he loved her; and so he burned in love that he was past himself in his reason; and forth toward night they yede unto supper, and Sir Gareth might not eat, for his love was so hot that he wist not where he was.

Sir Thomas Malory, Le Morte d'Arthur (c. 1470)

The contract between a knight and his lady was a combination of love, sacrifice and self-denial.

Guillaume IX, Count of Poitiers and Duke of Aquitaine (1071—1127), was a knight of the Crusades and one of the first troubadours, whose poems were among the earliest to celebrate the joys of romantic love:

No man can ever dream what that joy
Is like, neither by wishing or desiring it
Nor by thinking of it nor imagining it
Such a joy can never find its match
And he who would praise it worthily
Would not succeed in the space of a year.

Guillaume IX, Count of Poitiers, Les Chansons de Guillaume IX

The thoughts of a knight errant centred on military success and the art of courtly love.

An equally famous troubadour who succeeded Guillaume was Bernart de Ventadour (c.1140—1175). He was the son of a baker and alleged lover of Eleanor of Aquitaine, granddaughter of Guillaume IX. Eleanor later became Queen of England. Bernart's poems celebrate, once again, a joy d'amour, but in less bawdy fashion than his predecessor. For now the notion of sacrifice and self-denial becomes an important feature of the lyric:

Noble lady I ask of you
To take me as your servitor;
I'll serve you as I would my lord
Whatever my reward shall be.
Look, I am here at your command,
You who are noble, gay and kind
You are no bear or lion's whelp
Who'll kill me if I yield to you.

Bernart de Ventadour

The Provençal troubadours gave birth to the trouvères of the late twelfth and thirteenth centuries — among them Chrétien de Troyes and Conon de Béthune — who composed a more narrative and satiric form of verse. They also gave rise to the German lyric poets of the late twelfth to the fourteenth centuries, known as the Minnesingers, the most famous of whom were Gottfried von

Strassburg and Wolfram von Eschenbach. The legends of Arthur and the Knights of the Round Table were also developed at this time. Their origin may be traced to the Welsh historian Nennius, who was writing around AD 800. Geoffrey of Monmouth, a Benedictine monk working at Oxford in the twelfth century, drew on the records of Nennius when he wrote his Historia Regum Britanniae (c. 1136) which chronicled the events of the legendary King Arthur. The Arthurian legends greatly interested Eleanor of Aquitaine, and after she became Queen of England in the mid-twelfth century she saw to it that her host of southern poets exploited this narrative to the full.

But now lovely Kriemhild emerged like the dawn from the dark clouds, freeing from much distress him who secretly cherished her and indeed long had done so. He saw the adorable maiden stand there in all her splendour — gems past counting gleamed from her robe, while her rosy cheeks glowed bewitchingly; so that even if a man were to have his heart's desire he could not claim to have seen anything fairer.

The Niebelungenlied, c. 1200

Overleaf: *The chivalric code in relation to women meant that a knight's lady exerted as powerful an influence over him as his religion.*

The Elevation of Women

When the turmoil of the early Crusades had died down and knights began to spend less time on the battlefield, women increasingly provided the focus for their attentions. A state of relative military calm, coupled with the rise of the troubadour poets, dictated that feminine graces were no longer overlooked and women soon exerted a power over the knight as powerful as his religion. The highest glory of any knight was to be worthy of the love of the lady he desired. To this end, the most impressive acts of valour were performed and the most romantic adventures undertaken, in fiction at least, and to some extent in reality. Such a development in attitudes towards women was quite remarkable as compared to the earlier feudal period, when women were considered almost a burden; when marriage existed for the purposes of financial gain and women were simply delivered over to the highest bidder. Now women were the guiding lights of chivalry and the home evolved as a centre of social intercourse, promoting the civilizing arts of music, poetry, painting and sculpture.

Love is, of course, endlessly interesting. One of the remarkable developments of the twelfth century and later is the amount of time and space given to discussions of the ethics, and aesthetics, of sexual relationships. There was already, as we have seen, an interest in the psychology of love; and this developed, in some quarters, into courtly games, such as 'Courts of Love', in which the niceties of behaviour and morality might be discussed, often exploring the hypothetical situations set out in fashionable fiction, especially the newly popular romance form. Many views were possible: the discussion of love, and one assumes its practice, very soon becomes very complicated; for example, many of the troubadors did not seek to liberate women by sanctifying marriage, and opposed the idea that marriage was the proper consummation of love. Some claimed, seriously or not,

In the Middle Ages, Courts of Love encouraged the pleasures of extra marital relations above the constraints of marriage.

Comment vng seigr par son ange enuoia les trois fleurs de lis au roi en vng escu dazur au roy clouys.

that a woman could only find fulfilment in the love of a paramour who was not her husband — that, indeed, adultery was a prerequisite of a satisfactory, noble love affair. They argued that a knight should have a wife to whom he was committed for dynastic, political or business reasons — as was indeed most often the case — but also a 'goddess', whose commands he obeyed unhesitatingly.

> *Love cannot exert its powers between two people who are married to each other. For lovers give each other everything freely, under no compulsion of necessity, but married people are duty bound to give in to each other's desires.*
>
> Andreas Capellanus, *The Art of Courtly Love*

Capellanus' book is deliberately outrageous, however — a witty game taking over where Ovid's Ars Amatoria, that delightful manual of seduction, left off. But other writers, equally representative and influential, like Chrétien de Troyes, Capellanus' contemporary and fellow courtier in the court of Marie de Champagne, considered marriage the proper end of love. Yet he too recognizes the difficulty, and the necessity, of balancing the claims of marriage and devotion to one's lady with the claims of military fellowship and the winning of renown.

In the twelfth century, written tales of courtly love outlining a moral code of chivalric behaviour began to emerge.

Nature has a way of imitating art, and there is no doubt that such discussions and controversies round such ideals affected behaviour and conduct. Indeed, there is little doubt that the insistence on gallantry, on courtesy, on deference to the lady as the fount of honour, made many a marriage contracted for purely political reasons more tolerable for both parties than would otherwise have been the case. It may even be that, as often happens, what was pretended determinedly enough came to be, in fact, true.

Le premier chapitre du premier livre p
le de dieu le souverain·

n commencant
a declairer aua
nes choses des pro
priecez et des na
tures des choses
tant espirituelles
comme corporelles
Nous prendrons
nre commencement a cellui qui est co
mencement z fin de toute biens Et
au commencement nous Requerrons la
de du peir de lumere de qui vient tout
bien et tout don qui est parfait Et que
cellui qui enlumine tout homme qui
vient en ce monde et qui a tenebres
Reuelle les choses parsondes et les choses

nuclees amame a lumere Vueille me
ner a bonne consumacion ceste petite oeu
ure que a sa loenge et au prousst de ceulx
qui la liront lay recueillie et non pas sans
labour de diuers de des fame et des pro
phetes Le ije chapitre parle de lumere de
la diuine essence et de la pluralite des
t est donc personnes
si comme dit innocent En seul char
dieu pardurable sanz mesure no
muable tout puissant Le pere le fils et
le saint espirt troiz personnes en une
essence une substance et une nature si
ple en toute namere Le pere nest
de nullui Le fils est du pere tout seul
Le saint espirt est du pere z du fils
sanz commencement z sanz sin Le
pere est engendrant Le fils est naissant

The Court of Love

Two important women who considered gallantry an absolutely quintessential element to the practice of chivalry were Eleanor of Aquitaine and her daughter by her first husband, Louis VII of France, Marie de Champagne. Eleanor, as mentioned earlier, was a highly influential patron of the arts and it was largely her devotion to the troubadour which led to the immense popularity of courtly poetry during the Middle Ages. With the help of her daughter, Eleanor sought to convert gallant passion into a legitimate code of chivalric behaviour and began to legislate on matters of love at her court in Poitiers where cases were tried and judged as though presented before a tribunal.

From the 1160s onwards, Marie de Champagne continued her mother's work, both as patron of the arts and adjudicator at court at her home in Troyes. Marie's most famous literary protégé was Chrétien de Troyes, whose great romances included Tristan, Eric et Enide, Cligés and Lancelot. Her greatest contribution to the formalization of chivalric love was the commissioning of De Amore, translated in 1941 by J. J. Parry (and in 1989 by P. G. Walsh) as The Art of Courtly Love — a handbook of procedure in love written by her courtier Andreas Capellanus.

He was as handsome and attractive as Narcissus ...
His hair was like gold, and his cheeks like a young rose;
he had a well-shaped nose and a lovely mouth, and was
of as good a build as ever Nature could make.

Chrétien de Troyes, Cligés

True courtly love sought to reach beyond the boundaries imposed on it by medieval matrimony.

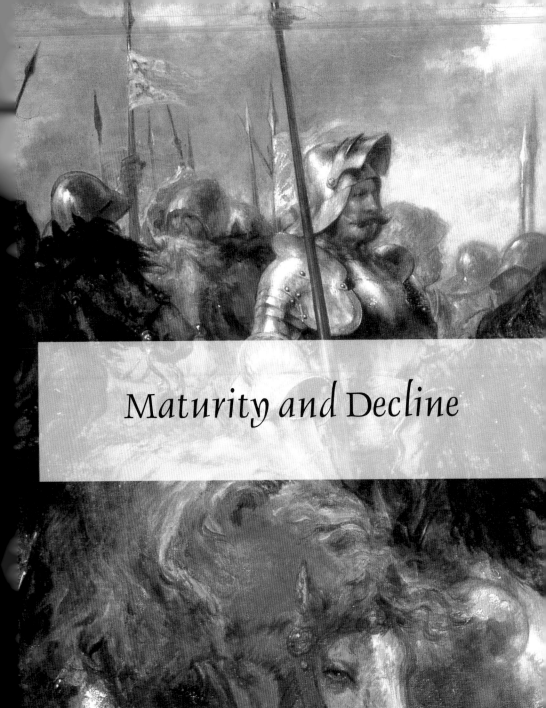

Maturity and Decline

Maturity and Decline

Chivalry was, in fact, a fraternal association, or rather an enthusiastic compact between men of feeling and courage, of delicacy and devotion — such, at least, was the noble aim it had in view, and which it constantly strove to attain.

Miller's 'Lectures on the Philosophy of History'

CHIVALRY WAS IN ITS VIGOUR during the religious wars of the Crusades which lasted roughly from 1100 to 1600. By the early fourteenth century, however, it was already showing evidence of decline, even though this was the period when it outwardly assumed its most magnificent form, particularly in England, under the auspices of Edward III and his immediate successors.

Edward was a great lover of the display and trappings of chivalry, and his reign saw the rise of heraldry, the widespread promotion of tournaments and banquets, the spreading fashion for courtly love, and an increase in the writing of great epic romances. It was during this period, up until the Wars of the Roses, that some of the most distinguished knights came to prominence: Sir Walter Manny, one of Edward III's most able commanders; Sir John Chandos, perhaps the most

The Chivalric Ideal reigned throughout two centuries of Holy Wars.

beloved knight of the Middle Ages; Bertrand du Guesclin, France's best-loved captain; and Edward the Black Prince, 'the chief flower of chivalry of all the world', according to the French chronicler, Froissart. At the age of fourteen Edward fought for his knightly spurs at the Battle of Crecy.

Towards the end of the golden age of chivalry, great importance was placed on the bestowing of Orders, such as those of the Garter, the Holy Spirit, the Golden Fleece and St James. These bound a knight and his sovereign in a personal bond of brotherhood, a bond in which all were equal and all bound to come to each other's aid. These Orders were an attempt to mobilize the ideology of chivalry in the service of politics now that feudal bonds were becoming so weak.

> *O! ye knights of England, where is the custom and usage of noble chivalry? What do ye now? but go to the bains to play at dice. Leave this, leave it and read the noble volumes of St Graal, of Lancelot, of Tristrem, of Galod, of Perceval, of Perceforest, of Gaw-ayn and many more; there shall ye see manhood, courtesy and gentilness.*

William Caxton, Book of the Order of Chivalry or Knighthood

The Decline of Chivalry

Several factors combined to undermine the substance and spirit of chivalry during the late Middle Ages. It may reasonably be argued that with the decline of the crusading ideal a serious decay was already well under way. To begin with, Pope Innocent III's declaration of a Crusade in 1208 against the Christian sect known as the Cathars living in southern France had the effect of decimating the birthplace of romantic chivalry as many thousands of these 'heretics' were mercilessly put to death. Diverting resources from the Holy Land unfortunately undermined the noble cause of Christian warfare, and this was compounded by the Pope's subsequent Crusades against his political enemies, including the German Emperor, Frederick II.

Louis IX's two disastrous Crusades of 1248—50 and 1267—70, followed by the rise of the Mamluks in Egypt and the siege of Acre in 1291, brought about a decline in the golden age of crusading (although crusades continued in Eastern Europe and the Mediterranean for generations to come). At this time, people also began to criticize the increasingly wealthy and perhaps corrupt Crusading Orders. The great wealth and military strength of these Orders now became a cause for concern and envy. In 1307 King Philip IV of France decreed the suppression of the Order of the Templars. Forty-five of its members were burned in one day in the city of Paris and its Grand Master, Jacques de Bourg-Molay, was also burned at the stake on charges of heresy.

Chivalry, in the full purity of its conception, was never realized; but it was an ideal of perfection in accordance with the notions of the times — to attain which every man might strive, and a standard by which others measured his actions — and as such its influence was immense.

John Wade, Women, Past and Present

During the fourteenth century, a great many political changes occurred which further accelerated the decline of chivalry. The feudal system of government which had allowed the noble class of independent knights to evolve was now being destroyed by the rise of sovereignty. Kings began to employ mercenary troops to defend their realms, judging the knight an unpredictable military force, unlikely to submit to periods of long service under the tight discipline of his sovereign. With the eruption of the Hundred Years War between France and England in 1338, the knight continued to lose out to the new breed of paid soldier. Even his weapons were becoming obsolete as gunpowder began to take the place of lance and sword. Suddenly the well-armoured knight, riding valiantly into battle for the love of his lady and the glory of chivalry, had lost his credibility. He took refuge in the tournaments, at one time an important field of training, yet now an elaborately staged pageant, hopelessly removed from the developments of modern warfare.

As the high ideals of the original crusading knight began to decline, many innocent people were put to death.

Some desperate attempts were made in the fifteenth century to revive the old codes of chivalry, but as the years progressed only traces of this lost institution remained. Religion no longer regulated the military spirit of men; knights had forfeited their ancient splendour and had become mere soldiers, while the art of gallantry had deteriorated into licentiousness.

Chivalry, in its maturity, teased out the virtues and vices of humanity. Yet the qualities of valour, steadfastness and justice, of courtesy, loyalty and obedience, although no longer publicly embraced, were never entirely forgotten. The noble aims of chivalry left an enduring mark on society, and it would be difficult for anyone to deny that modern courtesy is descended from the ideal of medieval chivalry — an ideal which proved as susceptible as any other to the perilous pitfalls of practice.

Opposite: *The knight as an independent ambassador of chivalry eventually lost his credibility and became merely a paid soldier.*
Overleaf: *Chaos and lawlessness re-emerged in the fourteenth century as the Crusades became political rather than religious in character.*

Suggested Further Reading

Barber, Richard, *The Knight and Chivalry*, London 1974

Batty, I., *Spirit and Influence of Chivalry*, London 1890

Capellanus, Andreas, *The Art of Courtly Love*, translation J. J. Parry, New York 1941

Cornish, F. W., *Chivalry*, New York 1901

Froissart, *Chronicles*, translation G. Brereton, London 1968

Gautier, Léon, *Chivalry*, London 1965

Harper-Bill, Christopher and Harvey, Ruth, *The Ideals and Practice of Medieval Knighthood*, Suffolk 1986

Hurd, Bishop, *Letters on Chivalry and Romance*, ed. E. J. Morley, London 1911

Jaeger, S. C., *The Origins of Courtliness: Civilising trends and the formation of Courtly Ideals 939—1210*, Philadelphia, 1985

James, G. P. R., *History of Chivalry*

Keen, Maurice, *Chivalry*, London 1984

Malory, Sir Thomas, *Le Morte d'Arthur*, c. 1470

Meller, Walter Clifford, *A Knight's Life in the Days of Chivalry*, London 1924

Prestage, Edgar, *Chivalry*, London 1928

Scaglione, Aldo, *Knights at Court: Courtliness, Chivalry and Courtesy from Ottonian Germany to the Italian Renaissance*, Berkeley, 1991

Stebbing, H., *History of Chivalry and the Crusades*, Edinburgh 1830

de Troyes, Chrétien, *Romances*, translation D. D. R. Owen

Illustration Notes

๛

Page 9 Detail from *The Overthrowing of the Rusty Knight* by Arthur Hughes. Courtesy of Christie's Images. Page 10 *Cavalry Skirmishes Between Crusaders and Turks* by Antonio Calza. Courtesy of Christie's Images. Pages 12-13 *Charlemagne's Vision of St James The Great*. Courtesy of Christie's Images. Page 15 *Parsifal in Quest of the Holy Grail* by Ferdiand Leeke. Courtesy of Christie's Images. Page 16 *Henri V d'Angleterre* (Bodleian Library, Oxford). Courtesy of Visual Arts Library. Page 19 Detail from *The Overthrowing of the Rusty Knight* by Arthur Hughes. Courtesy of Christie's Images. Pages 20-1 *Crossing the Rubicon* by Jean Fouquet (Louvre, Paris). Courtesy of Visual Arts Library. Page 22 *St George* by A. Mantegna (Academia, Venice). Courtesy of Visual Arts Library. Page 25 *Crossing the Rubicon* by Jean Fouquet (Louvre, Paris). Courtesy of Visual Arts Library. Page 26 *Elaine* by Edward Reginald Frampton. Courtesy of Christie's Images. Page 29 *Charlemagne's Vision of St James The Great*. Courtesy of Christie's Images. Pages 30-1 *St George Killing the Dragon* by Carpaccio (Scuola del Schiavoni, Venice). Courtesy of Visual Arts Library. Page 33 *King Louis of France Enters Antioch* by S. Mamerot. Courtesy of Visual Arts Library. Pages 34-5 Detail from *Christ on the Road to Calvary* by the Master of Astorga. Courtesy of Christie's Images. Page 37 *Christ on the Road to Calvary* by the Master of Astorga. Courtesy of Christie's Images. Pages 38-9 *Cavalry Skirmishes Between Crusaders and Turks* by Antonio Calza. Courtesy of Christie's Images. Page 41 *The Knight of the Sun* by Arthur Hughes. Courtesy of Christie's Images. Page 44 Detail from *the Triumph of St George* (Scuola Dalmata, Venice). Courtesy of Visual Arts Library. Page 47 *La Dame au Jardin* (Bodleian Library). Courtesy of Visual Arts Library. Pages 48-9 *History of Nastaglio de Onesti* by Botticelli (Museo del Prado, Madrid). Courtesy of Visual Arts Library. Page 51 *Jugement Dernier; Homme Priande* (Cleveland Museum of Art). Courtesy of Visual Arts Library. Page 52 *The Accolade* by Edmund Blair Leighton. Courtesy of Christie's Images. Page 55 *History of Nastaglio de Onesti* by Botticelli (Museo del Prado, Madrid). Courtesy of Visual Arts Library. Pages 56-7 *Queen of the Tournament* by Frank William Warwick. Courtesy of Christie's Images. Page 58 Detail from *The Overthrowing of the Rusty Knight* by Arthur Hughes. Courtesy of Christie's Images. Page 61 *Antiphonel of Marguerite de Baconel*. Courtesy of Christie's Images. Page 63 *Book of Hours* by The Boucicant Master Workshop. Courtesy of Christie's Images. Page 65 *Mariage de Foulques*. Courtesy of Visual Arts Library. Page 67 *God Speed* by Edmund Blair Leighton. Courtesy of Christie's Images. Pages 70-1 *St George and the Dragon* by Paolo Uccello (National Gallery, London). Courtesy of Visual Arts Library. Page 73 *Legend of the Fleur de Lys*. Courtesy of Visual Arts Library. Page 75 *Gospel Lectionary Single Leaf from Large Illuminated Manuscript*. Courtesy of Christie's Images. Page 76 *Marriage of Adam and Eve* by J. Corbechon (Fitzwilliam, Cambridge). Courtesy of Visual Arts Library. Pages 78-9 *Soldiers of the Holy Roman Empire Going into Battle* by Sir John Gilbert. Courtesy of Christie's Images. Page 80 *Martyrdom of the Pilgrims and Funeral of Ursula* by Carpaggio (Academia, Venice). Courtesy of Visual Arts Library. Page 85 *A Crusader Battle* by Antonio Calza. Courtesy of Christie's Images. Page 87 *Chroniques, Paris* by Jean Froissant. Courtesy of Christie's Images. Pages 88-9 *A Crusader Battle* by Antonio Calza. Courtesy of Christie's Images.

Index

❦

Index